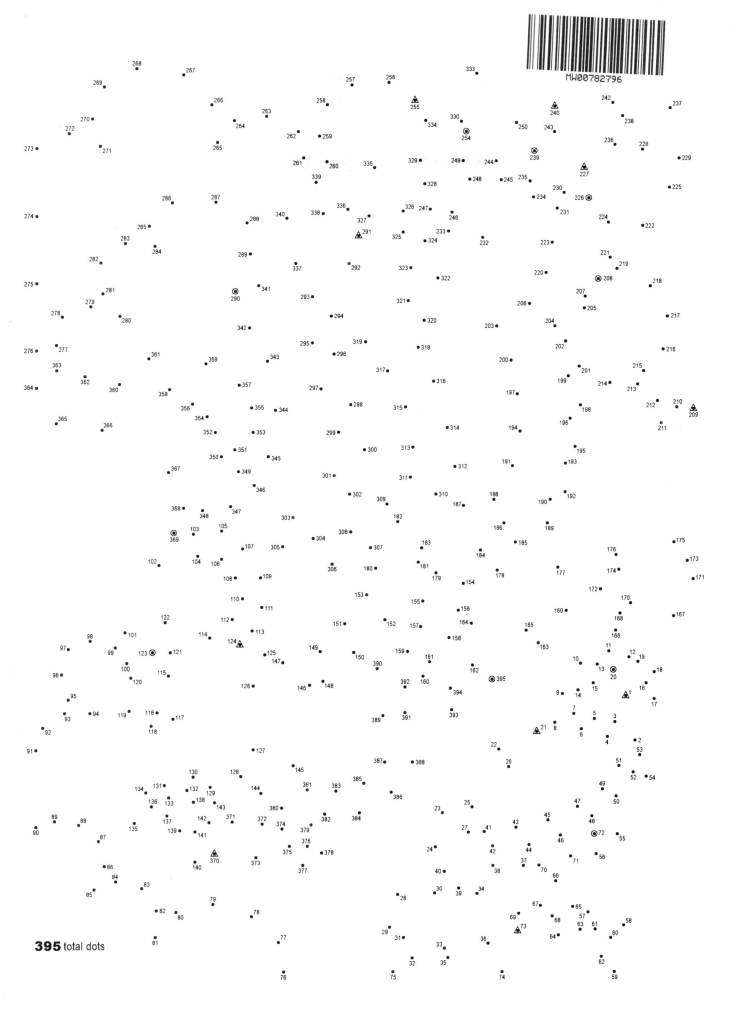

395 total dots

Plate 1

⚠ = Begin a new line section.

⊙ = Pick up your pen/pencil and look for the next sequential
number with the small triangle symbol next to it.

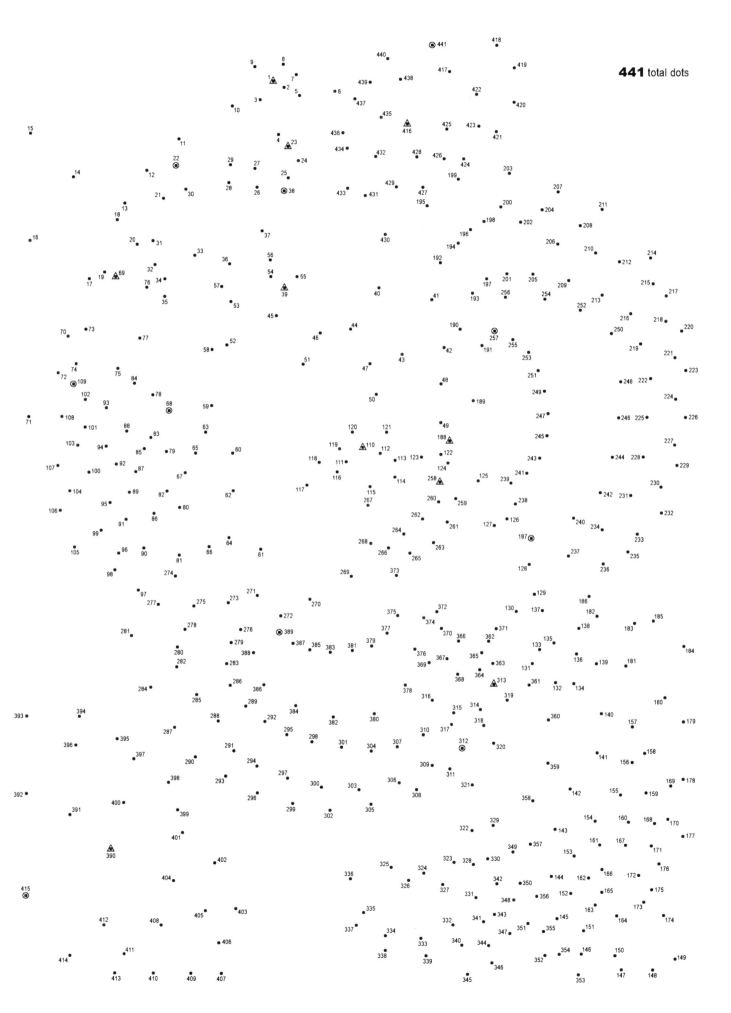

441 total dots

Plate 2

△ = Begin a new line section.

⊙ = Pick up your pen/pencil and look for the next sequential
number with the small triangle symbol next to it.

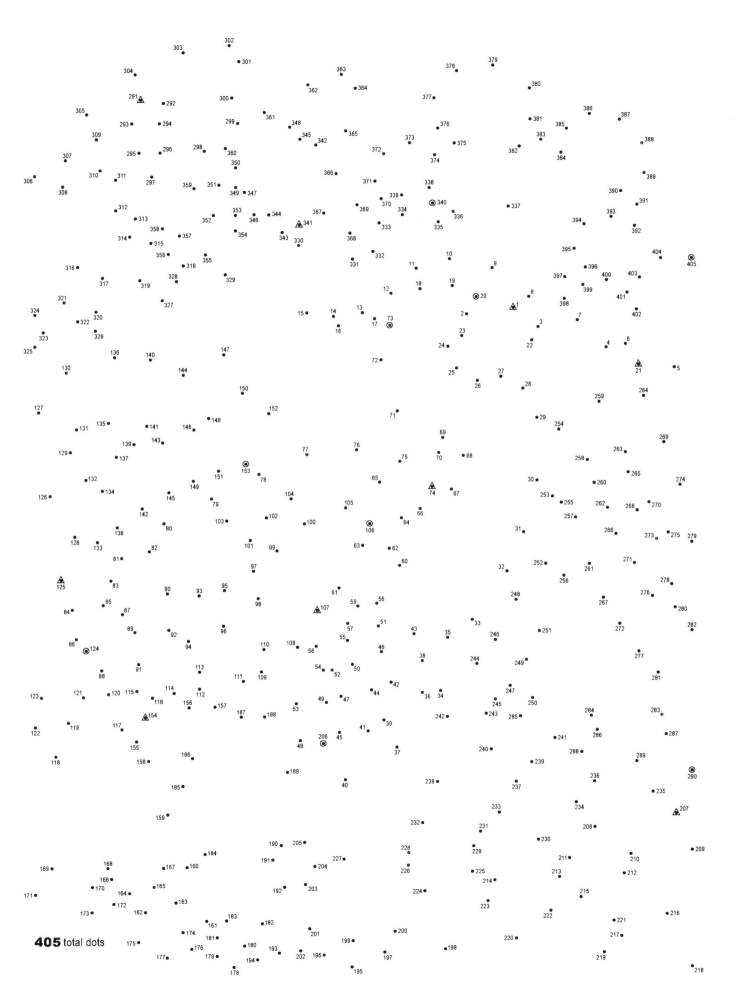

405 total dots

Plate 3

⚠ = Begin a new line section.

⊙ = Pick up your pen/pencil and look for the next sequential
number with the small triangle symbol next to it.

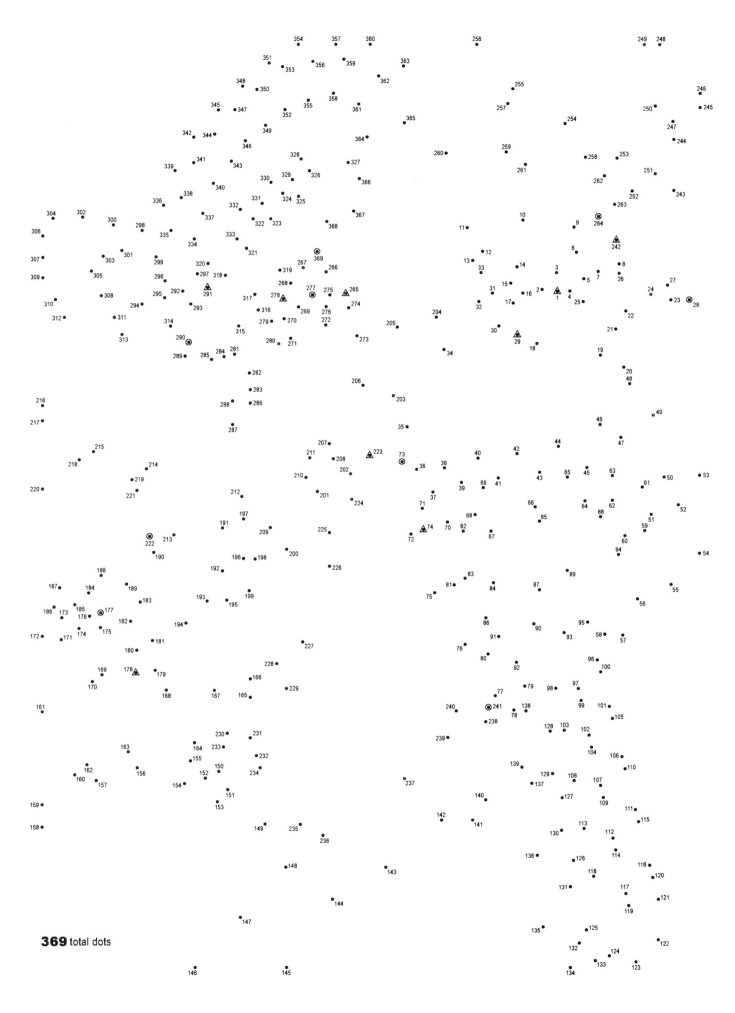

369 total dots

Plate 4

△ = Begin a new line section.

⊙ = Pick up your pen/pencil and look for the next sequential
number with the small triangle symbol next to it.

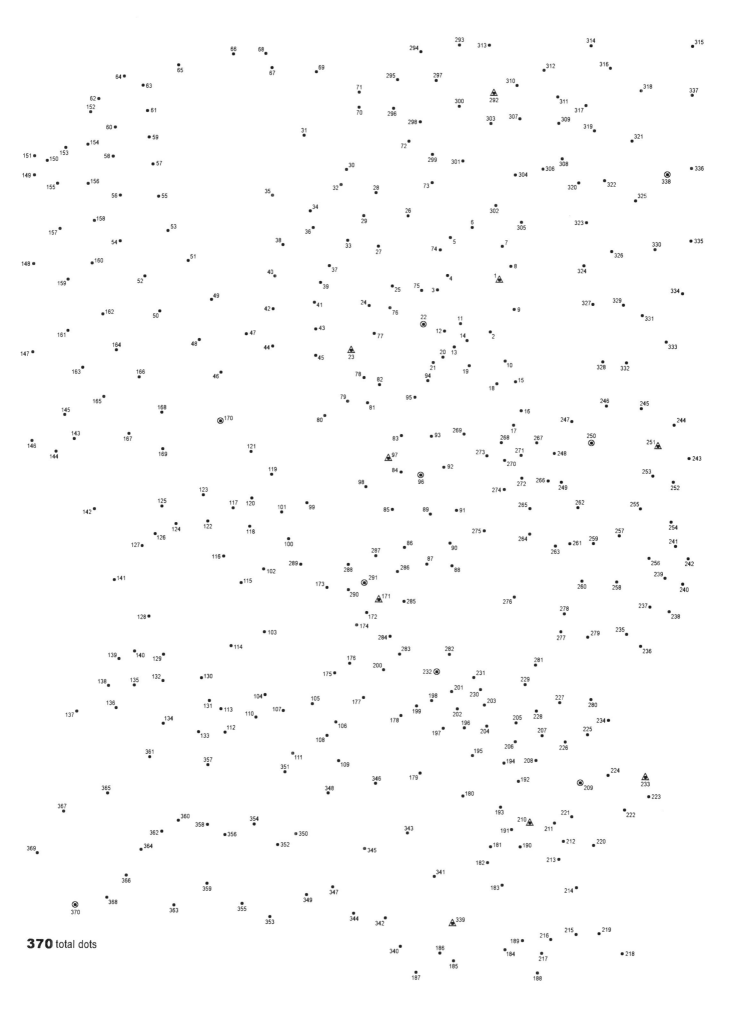

370 total dots

Plate 5

△ = Begin a new line section.

⊙ = Pick up your pen/pencil and look for the next sequential
number with the small triangle symbol next to it.

386 total dots

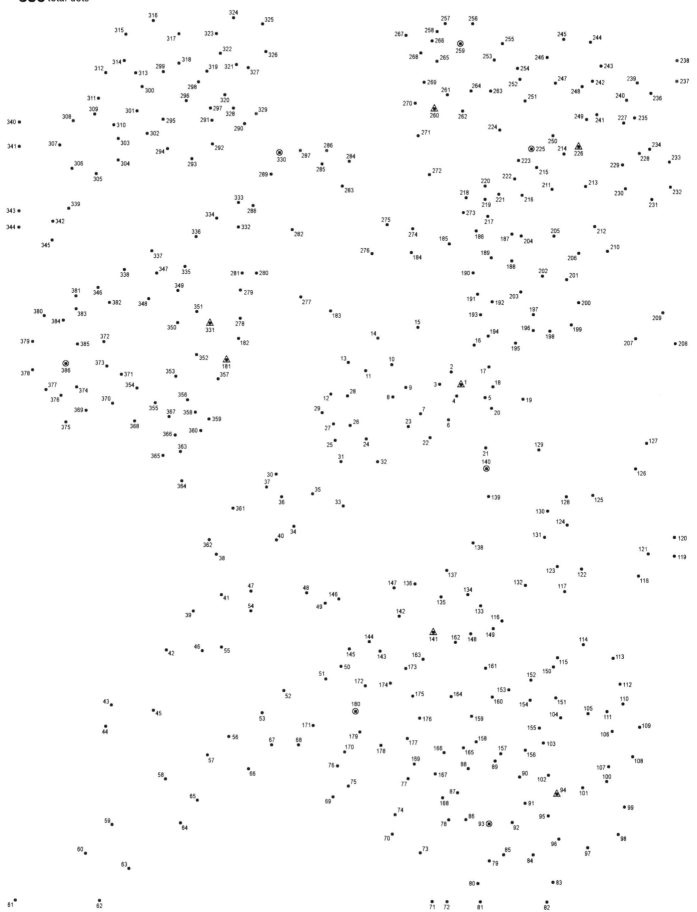

Plate 6

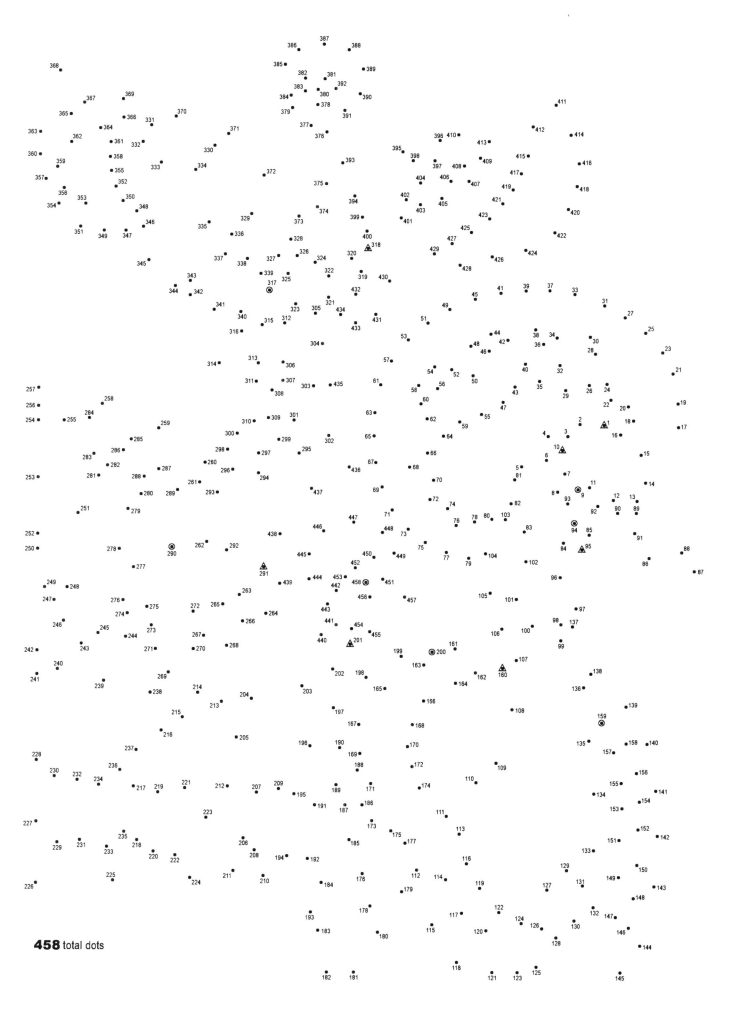

458 total dots

Plate 7

△ = Begin a new line section.

⊙ = Pick up your pen/pencil and look for the next sequential
number with the small triangle symbol next to it.

325 total dots

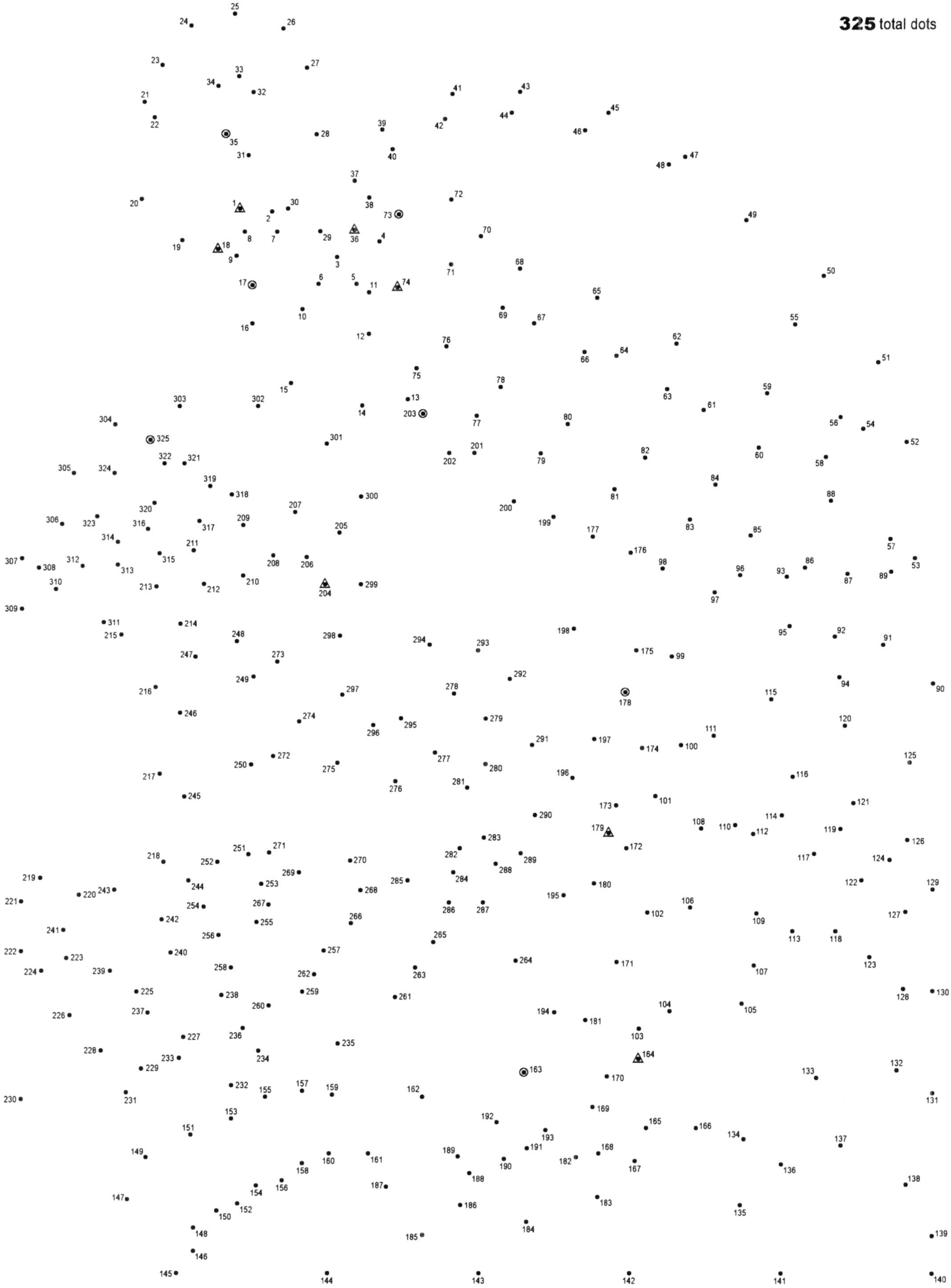

Plate 8

△ = Begin a new line section.

⊙ = Pick up your pen/pencil and look for the next sequential
number with the small triangle symbol next to it.

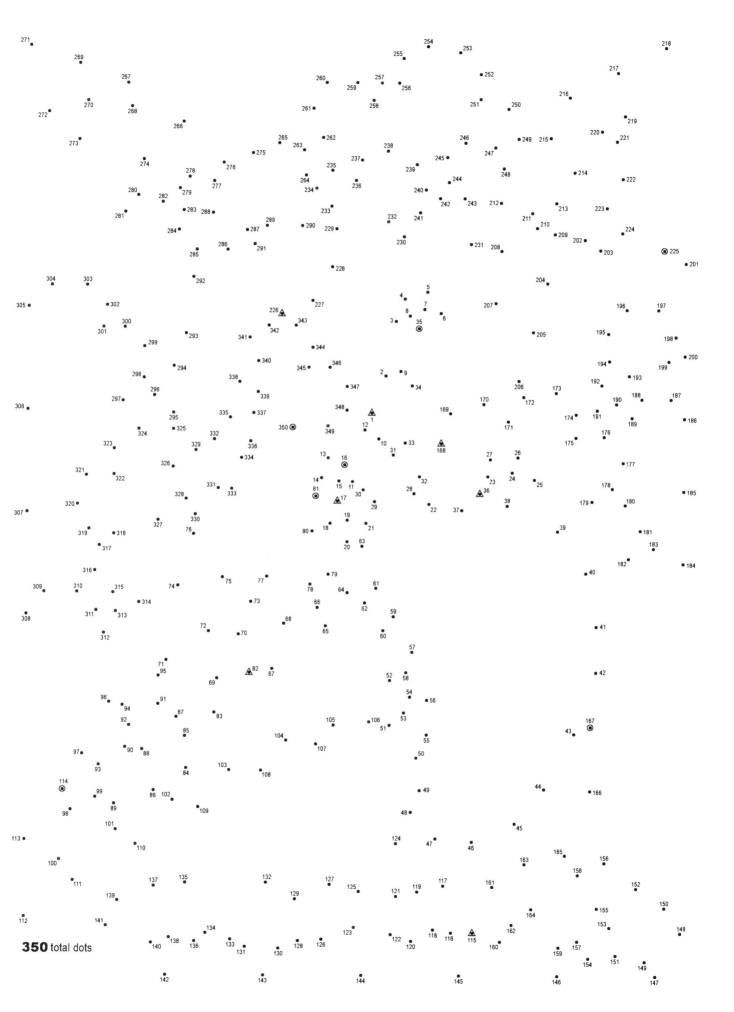
350 total dots

Plate 9

△ = Begin a new line section.

⊙ = Pick up your pen/pencil and look for the next sequential
number with the small triangle symbol next to it.

348 total dots

Plate 10

△ = Begin a new line section.

⊙ = Pick up your pen/pencil and look for the next sequential
number with the small triangle symbol next to it.

375 total dots

Plate 11

⚠ = Begin a new line section.

⊙ = Pick up your pen/pencil and look for the next sequential
    number with the small triangle symbol next to it.

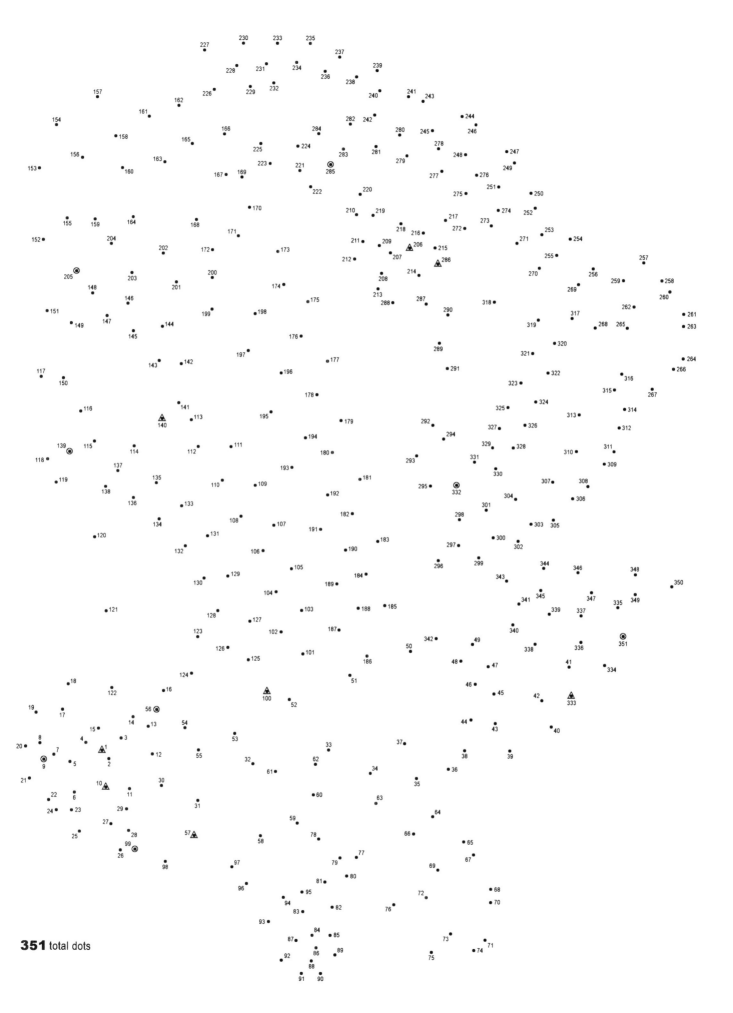

351 total dots

Plate 12

△ = Begin a new line section.

◉ = Pick up your pen/pencil and look for the next sequential
number with the small triangle symbol next to it.

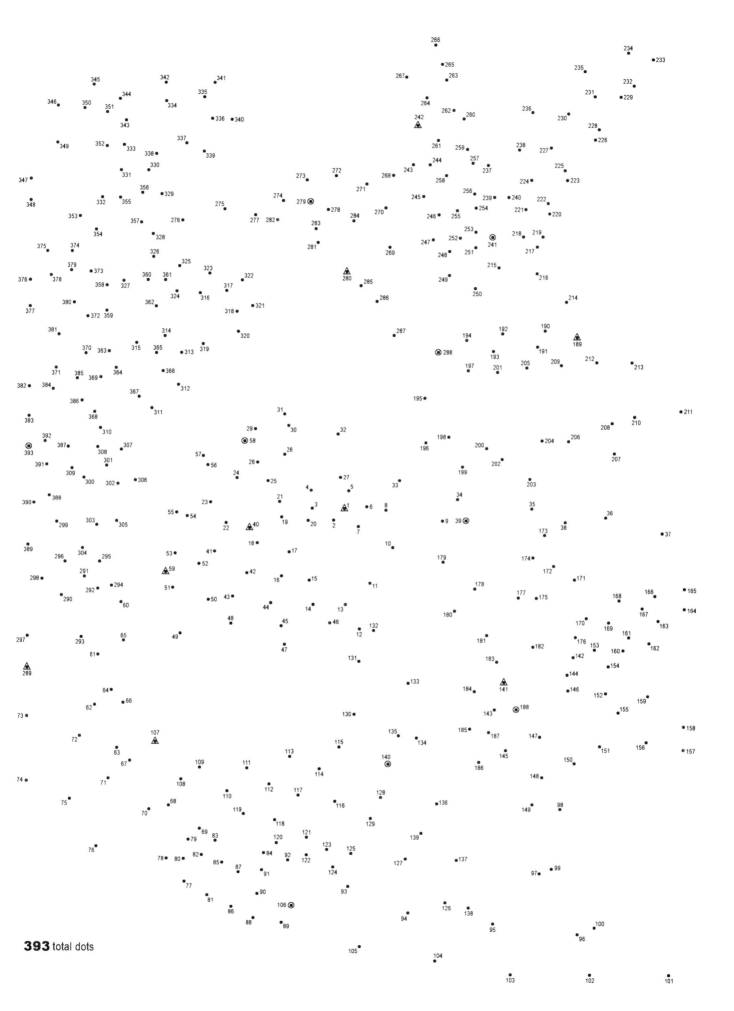

393 total dots

Plate 13

△ = Begin a new line section.

⊙ = Pick up your pen/pencil and look for the next sequential
number with the small triangle symbol next to it.

370 total dots

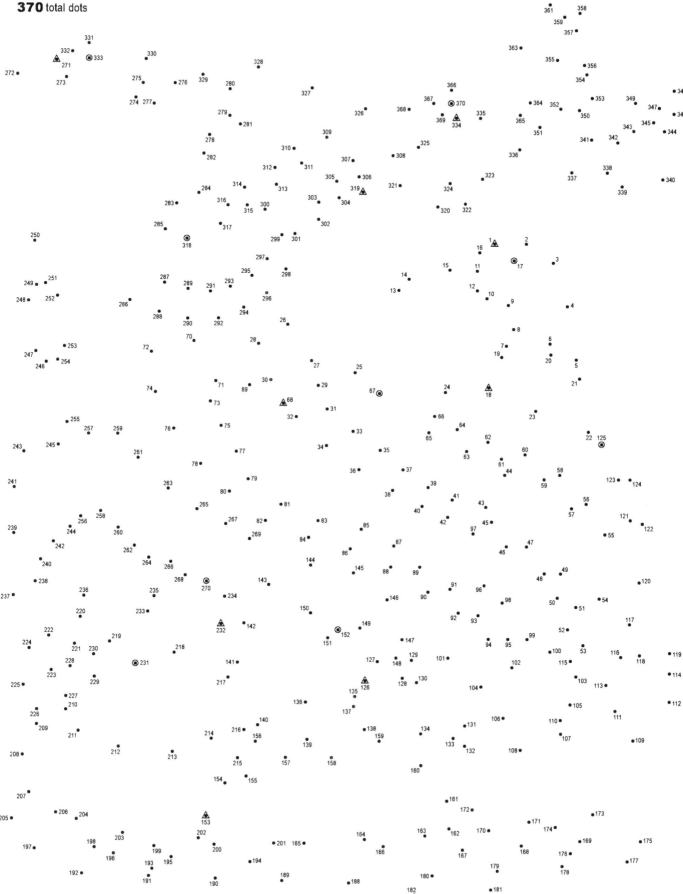

Plate 14

⚠ = Begin a new line section.

⊙ = Pick up your pen/pencil and look for the next sequential
number with the small triangle symbol next to it.

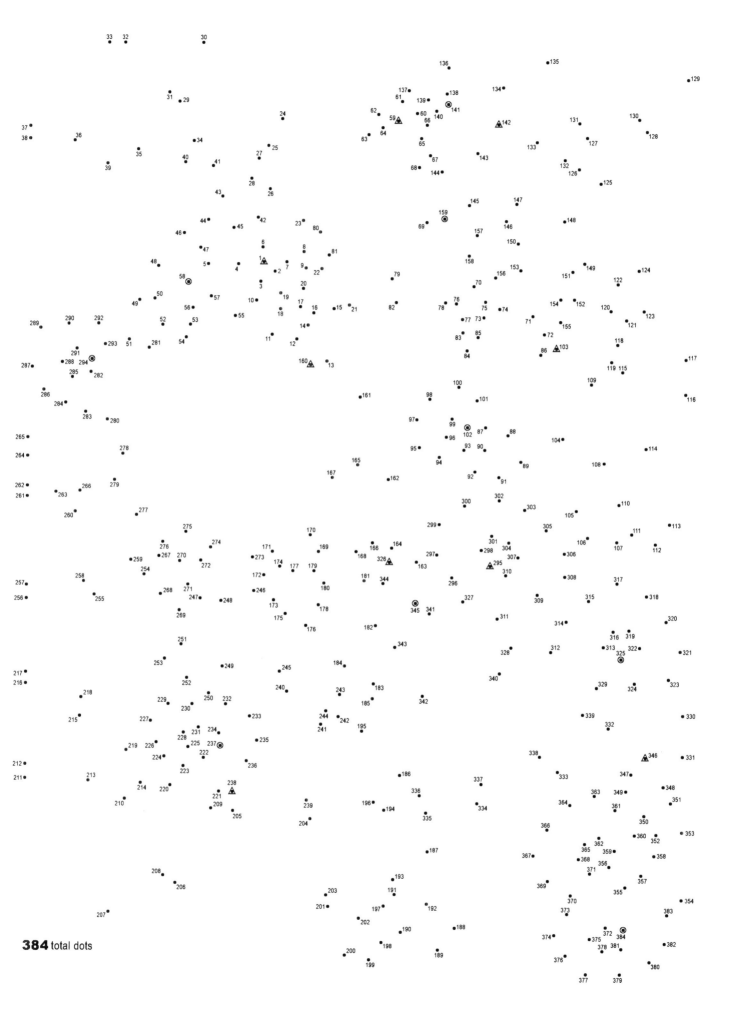

384 total dots

Plate 15

△ = Begin a new line section.

⊙ = Pick up your pen/pencil and look for the next sequential
number with the small triangle symbol next to it.

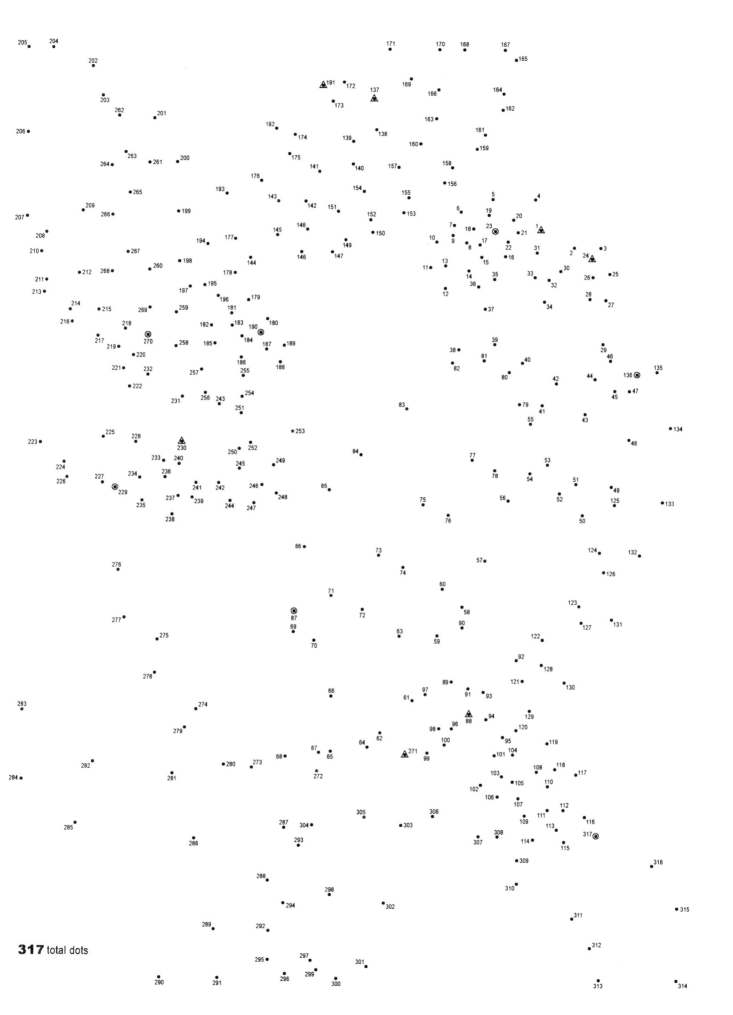

317 total dots

Plate 16

△ = Begin a new line section.

⊙ = Pick up your pen/pencil and look for the next sequential
number with the small triangle symbol next to it.

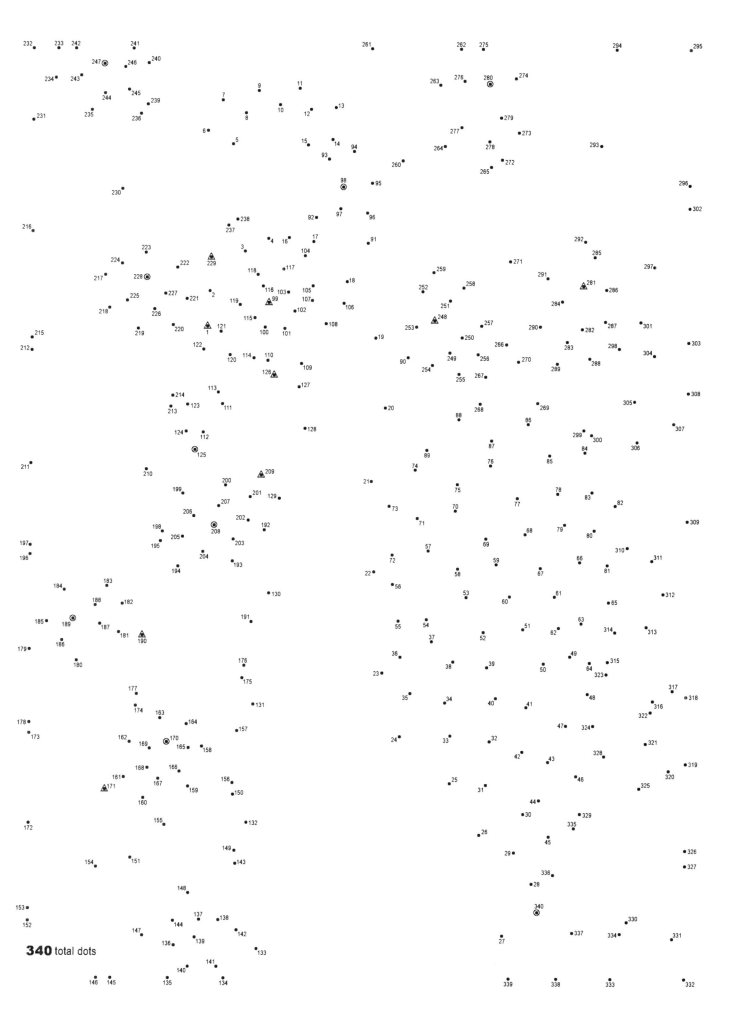

340 total dots

Plate 17

= Begin a new line section.

= Pick up your pen/pencil and look for the next sequential
number with the small triangle symbol next to it.

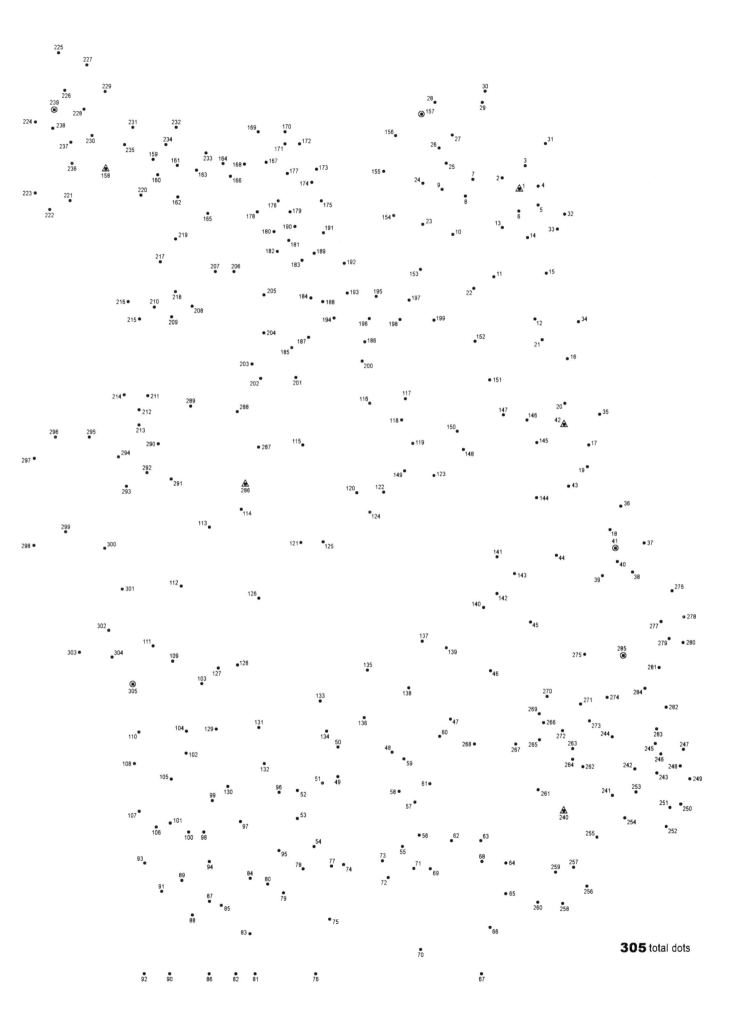

305 total dots

Plate 18

△ = Begin a new line section.

⊙ = Pick up your pen/pencil and look for the next sequential
    number with the small triangle symbol next to it.

320 total dots

Plate 19

△ = Begin a new line section.

⊙ = Pick up your pen/pencil and look for the next sequential
    number with the small triangle symbol next to it.

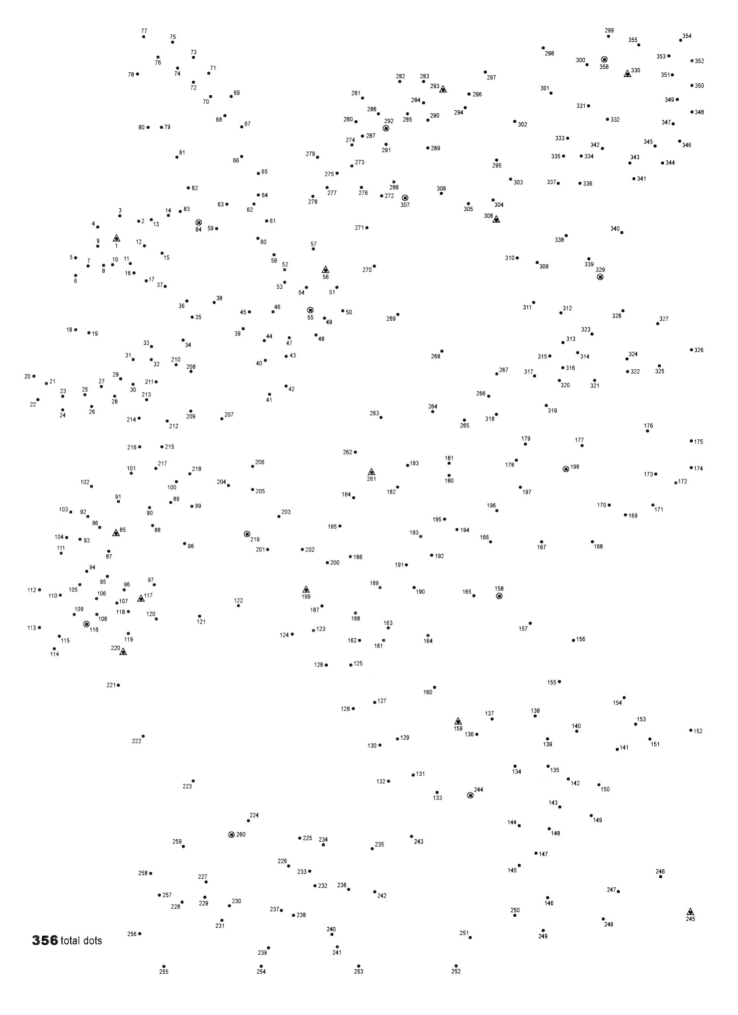

356 total dots

Plate 20

△ = Begin a new line section.

⊙ = Pick up your pen/pencil and look for the next sequential
number with the small triangle symbol next to it.

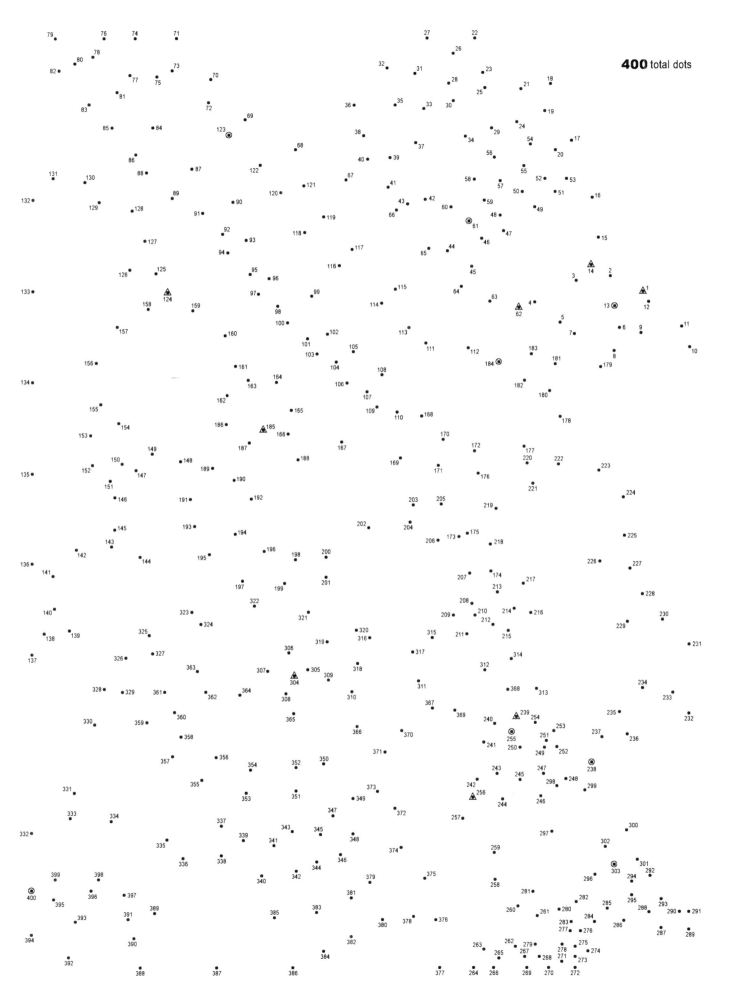

400 total dots

Plate 21

⚠ = Begin a new line section.

⊙ = Pick up your pen/pencil and look for the next sequential
number with the small triangle symbol next to it.

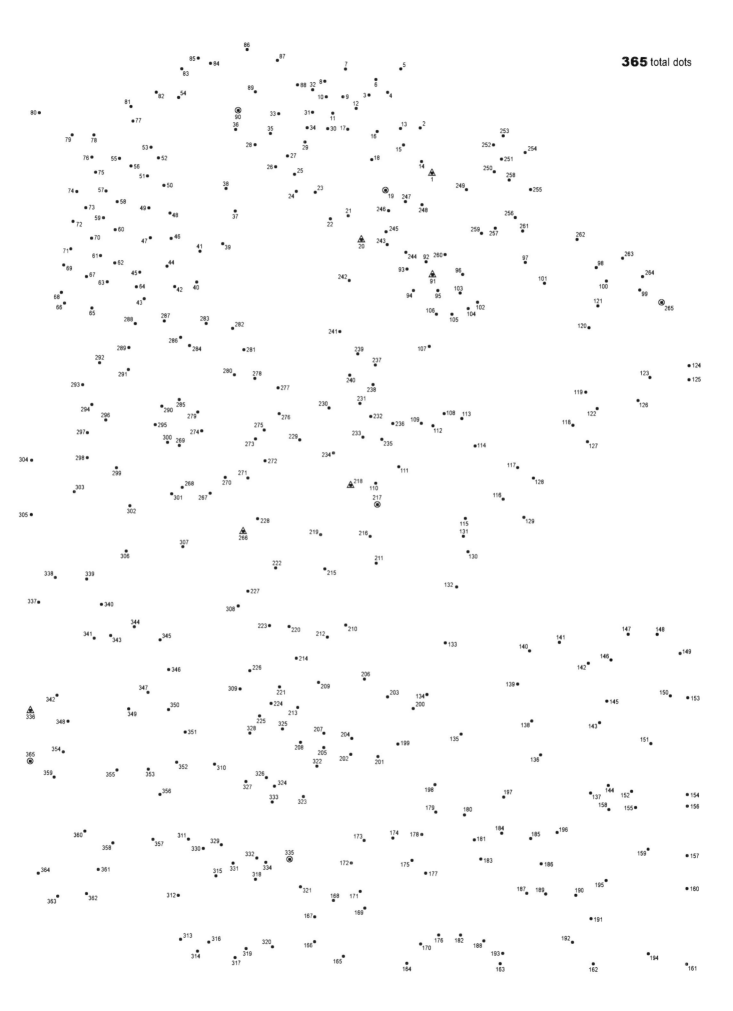

Plate 22

⚠ = Begin a new line section.

⊙ = Pick up your pen/pencil and look for the next sequential
number with the small triangle symbol next to it.

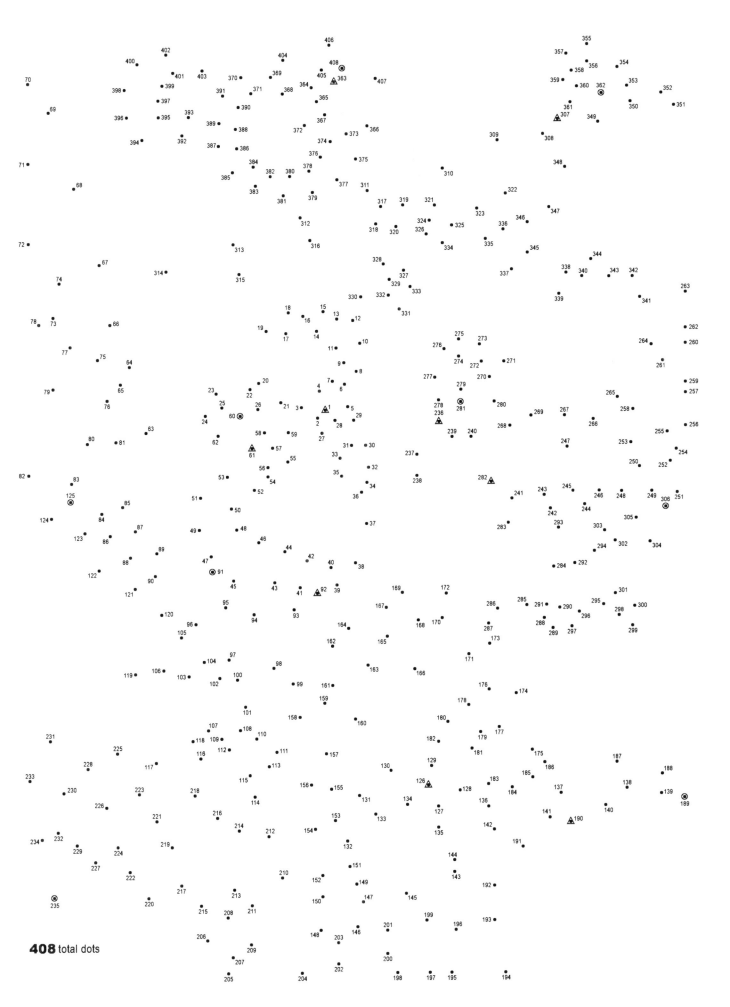

408 total dots

Plate 23

⚠ = Begin a new line section.

⊙ = Pick up your pen/pencil and look for the next sequential
number with the small triangle symbol next to it.

343 total dots

Plate 24

△ = Begin a new line section.

⊙ = Pick up your pen/pencil and look for the next sequential
number with the small triangle symbol next to it.

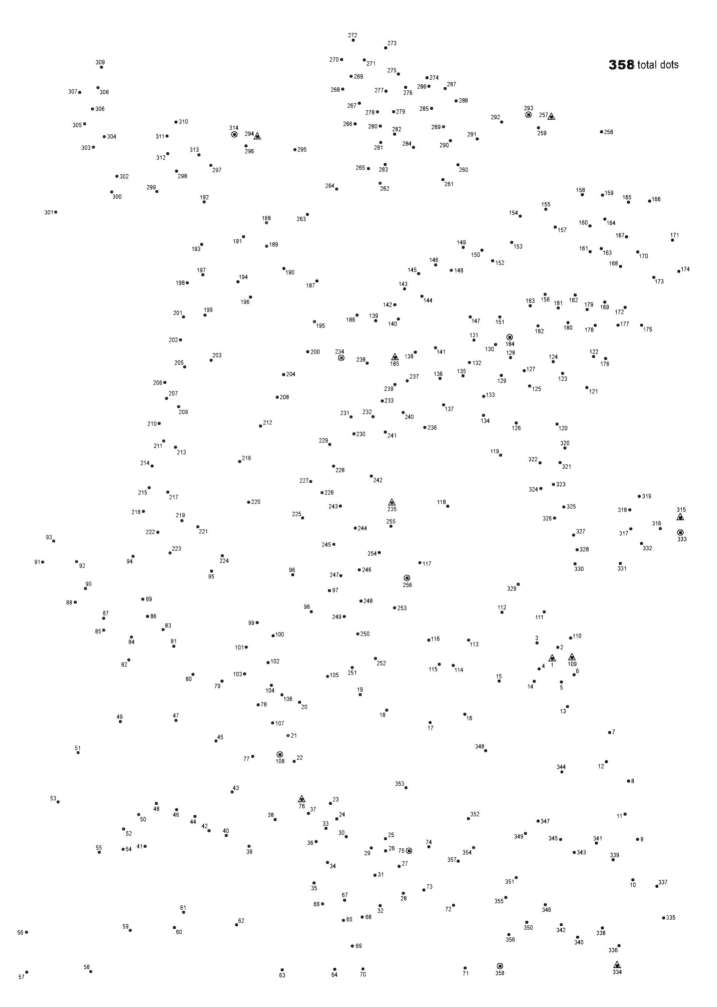
358 total dots

Plate 25

⚠ = Begin a new line section.

◉ = Pick up your pen/pencil and look for the next sequential
number with the small triangle symbol next to it.

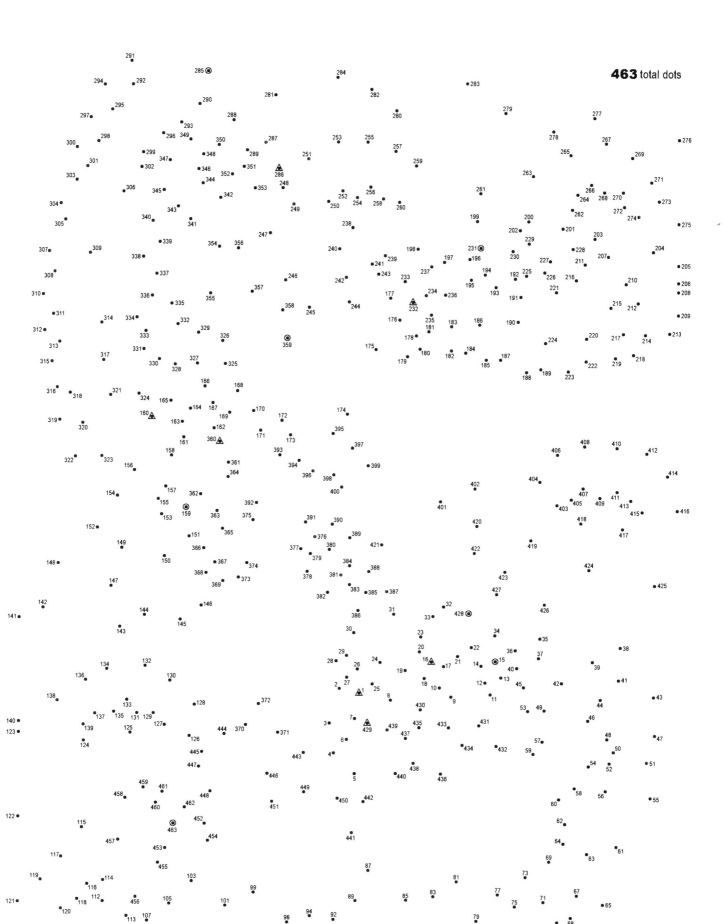

Plate 26

△ = Begin a new line section.

⊙ = Pick up your pen/pencil and look for the next sequential
    number with the small triangle symbol next to it.

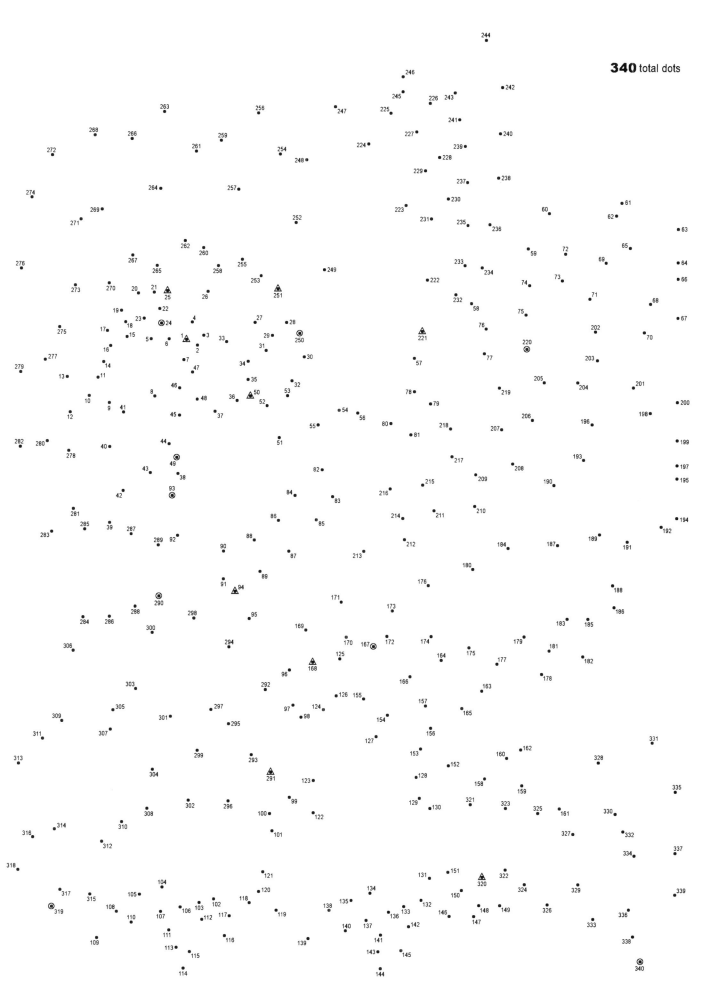

340 total dots

Plate 27

⚠ = Begin a new line section.

⊙ = Pick up your pen/pencil and look for the next sequential
number with the small triangle symbol next to it.

335 total dots

Plate 28

△ = Begin a new line section.

⊙ = Pick up your pen/pencil and look for the next sequential
number with the small triangle symbol next to it.

385 total dots

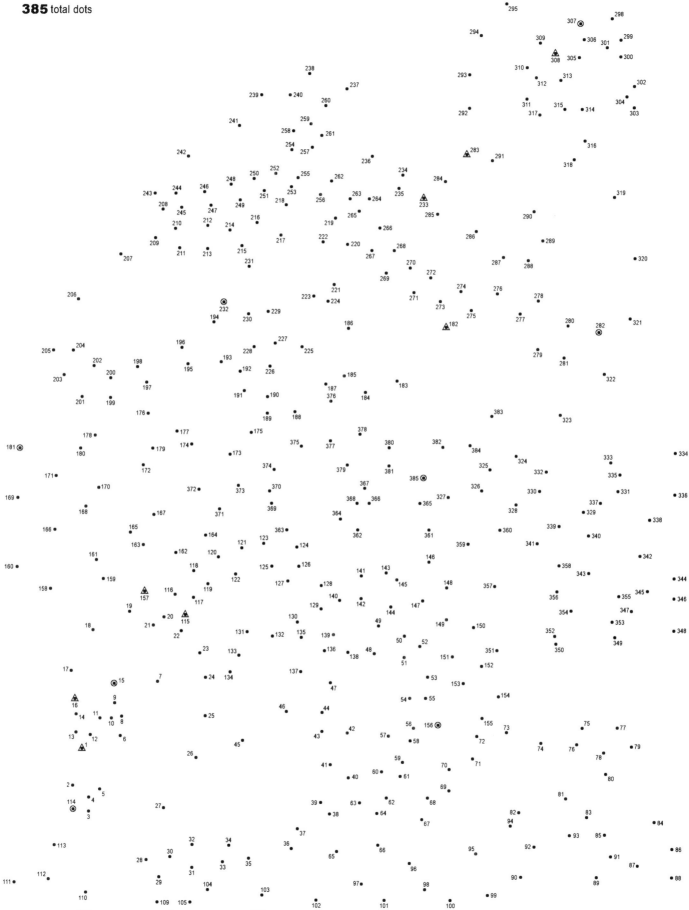

Plate 29

⚠ = Begin a new line section.

⊙ = Pick up your pen/pencil and look for the next sequential
number with the small triangle symbol next to it.

292 total dots

Plate 30

△ = Begin a new line section.

⊙ = Pick up your pen/pencil and look for the next sequential
number with the small triangle symbol next to it.

SOLUTIONS

Plate 1 — Bald Eagle

Plate 2 — Bird of Paradise

Plate 3 — Blue Heron

Plate 4 — Blue Jay

Plate 5 — Cassowary

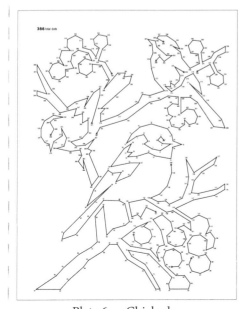

Plate 6 — Chickadee

Plate 7 — Crowned Crane

Plate 8 — Flamingo

Plate 9 — Frigatebird

Plate 10 — Great Curassow

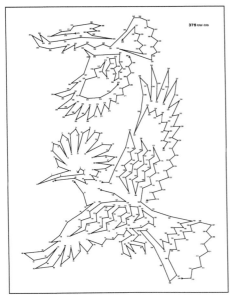

Plate 11 — Hoopoe

Plate 12 — Horned Owl

Plate 13 — Hummingbird

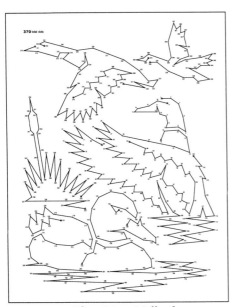

Plate 14 — Mallard

Plate 15 — Northern Cardinal

Plate 16 — Osprey

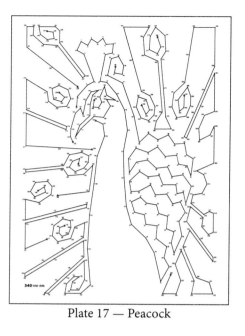

Plate 17 — Peacock

Plate 18 — Pelican

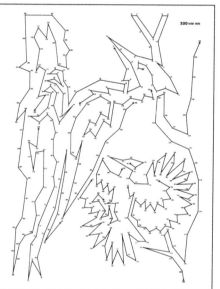

Plate 19 — Pileated Woodpecker

Plate 20 — Puffin

Plate 21 — Raven

Plate 22 — Rhinoceros Hornbill

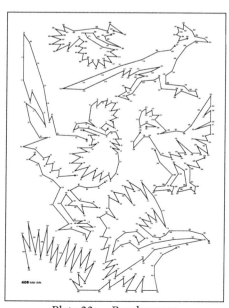

Plate 23 — Roadrunner

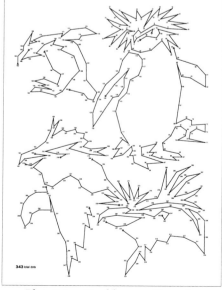

Plate 24 — Rockhopper Penguin

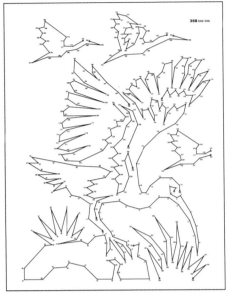

Plate 25 — Scarlet Ibis

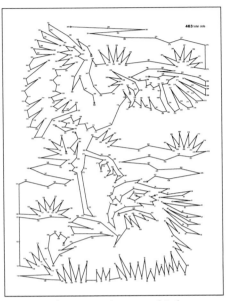

Plate 26 — Secretarybird

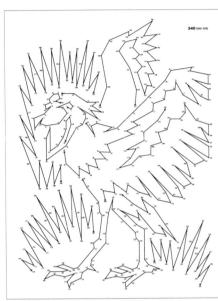

Plate 27 — Shoebill

Plate 28 — Spoonbill

Plate 29 — Swan

Plate 30 — Tragopan